One World, One Day

Barbara Kerley

NATIONAL GEOGRAPHIC
WASHINGTON, D C

At dawn, as the sun slips over the horizon,

kids around the world

get up

wash up

Porridge

Pancakes

Churros

Toast

Hot sweet tea with plenty of milk
Lots of things taste good for breakfast.

Time for school. Don't be late!

But by bus

The trip can be a short walk or a real adventure.

by bike

on foot
on time
kids come ready to learn.

Reading

Writing

Music

Math

Science projects

Arts and crafts

Recess rocks!

And so does lunch.

A little more learning.

Then kids stand up, clean up

and head
    for home

any way they can.

School is over, but the day is hardly done.

Kids work.

Kids play

with bats and balls

and hoops

and slides.

They do homework, chores, or nothing at all,

pondering life's big questions, like...

What's for dinner?

Veggies

Pasta

Chicken

Rice

Big round pizzas with plenty of cheese
Lots of things taste good for dinner.

The sun is setting.

Families gather

on the porch

by the fire.

Family time.

Quiet time.

Time to brush teeth.

Time for one more story.

Kiss goodnight.
Lights out.

Around the world

kids dream of tomorrow

and all the possibilities

of just

one day.

FROM 1981 THROUGH 1983, I lived in Nepal, in a small village a day's walk from the motor road. I was working there as a Peace Corps volunteer, teaching math, science, and English.

For much of that time, I lived with a Nepali family—a mom, dad, and three kids. Some aspects of their lives were decidedly different from what I'd experienced in America: the house had no electricity; the family's mom cooked on an open-hearth fire on the kitchen's dirt floor; and one of the oldest son's chores was milking the family water buffalo. But much about their lives was very familiar to me. The kids got up every morning, went to school, came home, helped around the house, and the whole family gathered in the evening to relax and spend time together.

The school where I taught had no electricity, but there was recess, school assemblies, and a faculty who taught lessons and gave quizzes. Life in my village was different than my life in America, but in a lot of ways, not *that* different. Instead, my experience in Nepal—and the traveling I've done in the 25 years since then—convinced me that all of us around the world have much in common, and that the more we can embrace our commonality, the more tolerant we can be of our differences.

That is the spirit behind this book. Kids in countries around the world have days remarkably similar to each other, in the ways that really matter. Kids go to school, they play, they spend time with their families. This book represents one day, from sunrise to sunset, around the world—a day we share together.

Cover
Location: The outskirts of Phnom Penh, CAMBODIA
Caption: A boy balances as he walks on a railroad track home from school. A weekly train carries passengers and cargo down the line.
Photographer's Note: One evening in Cambodia on the railway track from Phnom Penh to Battambang, on which Cambodia's last and only passenger train runs, I saw this boy, walking away from me, back home from school. He was oblivious of my presence, totally lost in concentration. He was swaying to and fro, balancing with his arms like a tightrope walker's. The light conditions were perfect. The sun reflected onto the tracks, which made them seemingly disappear into the horizon. Suddenly there was the perfect picture.
Credit Line: Nigel Dickinson

Half-title, p. 1
Location: Dembel Jumpora, GUINEA-BISSAU
Caption: Children share rice from a communal bowl. In addition to rice, farmers in Guinea-Bissau also grow corn, cashews, and peanuts.
Credit Line: Ami Vitale

Title Page, pgs. 2-3
Location: Amarapura, Mandalay, MYANMAR
Caption: Spanning Taungthaman Lake, the U Bein Bridge serves as a major passageway for people in the area.
Photographer's Note: For over two centuries hundreds of local villagers have made the daily journey across this famous bridge, the longest teak bridge in the world. I found walking across the slippery wooden bridge in the wind a difficult and scary process—even if the locals did make it look easy. Women going to market, children off to school, monks visiting the nearby temple, and men going to work all make up the rhythm of traffic that flows by. The bridge makes life here possible and I tried to capture that.
Credit Line: Bernard Narthine/Lonely Planet

Pgs. 4-5 "At dawn"
Location: Kerala, INDIA
Caption: A lagoon is a peaceful spot for morning prayer.
Credit Line: Harry Gruyaert/Magnum Photos

Pg. 6 "Get up"
Location: St. Louis, Missouri, USA
Caption: Two sisters in pajamas jump on a big, soft bed.
Credit Line: FK PHOTO/Corbis

Pg. 6 "Wash up"
Location: Dembel Jumpora, GUINEA BISSAU
Caption: A boy enjoys a refreshing scrub. During the rainy season in Guinea-Bissau, water is plentiful.
Photographer's Note: For six months, I lived in a small village called Dembel Jumpora in the West African country of Guinea-Bissau. The boy washing, Alio, was swimming in a tufe—a sinkhole created to collect the rainwater—a sight seen at the end of the dry season. Alio got ahold of my soap, loved the bubbles it made, and got a little exuberant lathering up. On my last evening sitting under a sea of stars talking with the children, Alio asked lots of questions. "Do you have mango trees like we do? Cashews?" Later he innocently asked if we had a moon in America. It seemed so symbolic and touching that he should feel like America was a separate world, and reminded me that we are all tied together in an intricate web on this planet, whether we believe it or not.
Credit Line: Ami Vitale

Pg. 7 "Celebrate a new day"
Location: Kadesh Barnea, ISRAEL
Caption: A warm sun casts shadows on the walls as Sudanese refugee children play in Kadesh Barnea. The village lies in a great desert valley.
Photographer's Note: On a warm summer day in southern Israel near the Israel-Egypt border, I was looking for refugees from Darfur. The information I gathered the day before took me to the tiny Israeli village of Kadesh Barnea, where the locals hosted dozens of refugees, all women and children from Sudan. The refugee set-up was minimal but very clean and cozy. The men were in Tel Aviv working and looking for homes for their families. Everybody looked healthy and happy and many had amazing stories about their trip from Darfur to Israel, through Egypt. I was there for a few hours watching the children play. We shared a meal. I left the village with a very positive feeling.
Credit Line: Yannis Behrakis/Reuters

Pg. 8 "Porridge"
Location: Wonsan, NORTH KOREA
Caption: Porridge with soy milk is a hot and filling breakfast for this young girl in North Korea.
Photographer's Note: I went to North Korea to cover a humanitarian project sponsored by the Rotary International and First Steps, a Canadian organization, in October 2007. The program is helping to feed 40,000 North Korean orphans each day all over the country. We went to this orphanage in a town called Wonsan. There were around 150 orphaned children and babies eating breakfast in a darkly lit room. There is very little electricity in the country. There is very little food for that matter, but this basic meal of porridge mixed with with soy milk is a daily life saver to these orphaned children. After breakfast they practiced gymnastics and patriotic singing and dancing in a traditional Korean style.
Credit Line: Mark Pearson

Pg. 8 "Pancakes"
Location: Sevierville, Tennessee, U.S.A.
Caption: A hungry young boy tackles a towering stack of pancakes dripping with syrup and melted butter.
Credit Line: Jeff Greenberg/PhotoEdit

Pg. 8 "Churros"
Location: Granada, Andalucia, SPAIN
Caption: A girl enjoys a breakfast of churros, a crunchy fried doughnut popular in Spain. Churros are eaten plain or rolled in cinnamon sugar.
Credit Line: Martin Moos/Lonely Planet

Pg. 8 "Toast"
Location: Cremorne, New South Wales, AUSTRALIA
Caption: A girl starts her day with a warm slice of toast. Kids in Australia eat toast topped with butter and jam, or sometimes, topped with baked beans and bacon.
Credit Line: David Woolley/Digital Vision/Getty Images

Pg. 9 "Hot sweet tea"
Location: Azmiriganj, BANGLADESH
Caption: A boy helps his family by working in a restaurant pouring tea. In South Asia, many people drink tea with milk and sugar.
Photographer's Note: Roki makes tea in a restaurant in the main Bazaar in Azmiriganj, a remote town, in Bangladesh. Roki studied up to grade four, but quit school to help his three sisters and his aging mother. He described his day to me. "I wake up at 6:00 am, brush and wash dirty dishes in the river behind the restaurant. Then I make tea until afternoon. Later I have a bath. For dinner I have rice with potato. After that I go back to work, usually until 9:00 pm, and then I go to sleep." Roki has stepped up to his responsibilities to his family, but I hope he will be able to continue his education someday.
Credit Line: Shehzad Noorani/Peter Arnold, Inc.

Pgs. 10-11 "Time for school"
Location: Ahmadabad, Gujarat, INDIA
Caption: A row of children in a refugee camp are ready to start the day's lessons.
Photographer's Note: During the months of horribly violent Hindu/Muslim riots in Gujarat, India, early in 2002, I took this picture of Muslim children inside a camp for displaced people. They were wonderful and full of laughter despite the terrible conditions. Children are amazing in the way they adapt to whatever situation is put in front of them. They were happy to show me around their new home, which consisted of classrooms filled with people. They helped me see that there is always joy in the most miserable places.
Credit Line: Ami Vitale

Pg. 12 "Short walk"
Location: Jodhpur, Rajasthan, INDIA
Caption: A girl races up a set of steps. Jodhpur is sometimes called the Blue City because of the many blue houses nestled around Mehrangarh Fort.
Credit Line: Bruno Morandi

Pg. 12 "Real adventure"
Location: The Nu River between Biluoshan and Gaoligongshan, Gongshan County, Yunnan Province, CHINA
Caption: A zip line over the Nu River makes for an exciting trip to school.
Photographer's Note: This part of China, which lies between southeast Tibet and northern Myanmar, is the last frontier in the country and still remote. The Nu River with its

flanking mountain ranges—Biluoshan on the left bank and Gaoligongshan on the right—still has many of these suspension bridges. Here a young woman uses the cable to cross from her house seen in the distance to the other side of the river to access the road. Transportation is still in its early stages. Not too long ago the roads were just pony tracks. For centuries the only way to cross the rivers was by rope-bridge or rattan suspension bridge. This area is home to Lisu, Nu, and Dulong ethnic minorities as well as Han people who migrated there in recent years.
Credit Line: Pete Oxford

Pg. 12 "By bus"
Location: Doylestown, Pennsylvania, U.S.A.
Caption: A girl waves from the back window of a school bus. All across America, kids ride bright yellow buses to school.
Credit Line: Tom Grill/Corbis

Pg. 13 "By bike"
Location: A very small village on the outskirts of the town of Oruro, Oruro Department, BOLIVIA
Caption: Children ride sturdy bicycles down a dusty road to get to school.
Credit Line: Anders Ryman/Corbis

Pg. 13 "On foot"
Location: Hani village, Huangchaoba near the town of Yuanyang in Honghe Prefecture, Yunnan Province, CHINA
Caption: A long line of children in the Chinese highlands cross terraced rice fields as they walk to school.
Photographer's Note: Children are on their way to school using the dividing walls between the rice terraces as walkways. The Yi people are the second largest ethnic group in the highlands of Ailaoshan. Together with the Hani people, they built some of the terraces. Until about 6 years of age, the Yi children wear very decorated outfits, including hats that are adorned with coins and chains.
Credit Line: Pete Oxford

Pg. 14 "Reading"
Location: Bahati, near the village of Malindi, KENYA
Caption: A boy pores over a book at his small village school. In Kenya, schoolchildren learn to read both English and Kiswahili.
Credit Line: Nick Cobbing/Alamy Ltd

Pg. 14 "Writing"
Location: Hani village, Huangchaoba near the town of Yuanyang in Honghe Prefecture, Yunnan Province, CHINA
Caption: A young girl begins to master the art of writing Chinese. Children learn how to combine a series of strokes, hooks, and dots to make thousands of different characters.
Credit Line: Pete Oxford

Pg. 14 " Music"
Location: Shanghai, CHINA
Caption: A boy stretches to reach just the right note while playing a Chinese lute.
Photographer's Note: I was working in Shanghai in the mid-1980s, and journalists and photographers working in China were closely monitored. The government assigned me a "minder" who accompanied me everywhere, telling me what I could and could not photograph. This, of course, was quite frustrating to a photographer used to wandering freely in democratic societies. Plus, the "minder" would insist that I photograph certain situations that would show China in its best light. When they took me to a music school I was reluctant, because these staged "photo ops" are usually stilted and boring. But when I saw this child struggling with an instrument about the same size as he was, I was completely charmed, and recognized emotions on his face that anyone in any culture could understand.
Credit Line: Jodi Cobb/National Geographic

Pg. 15 "Math"
Location: Sussex, Freetown Peninsula, SIERRA LEONE
Caption: A young boy studies his times tables at school. As tension from the civil war has decreased, many more schools are reopening.
Credit Line: Christopher Herwig/Getty Images

Pg. 15 "Science projects"
Location: Hermosa Beach, California, U.S.A.
Caption: A girl takes careful notes while conducting a science lab. Plastic goggles protect her eyes.
Credit Line: Hill Street Studios/Blend Images/Getty Images

Pg. 15 "Arts and crafts"
Location: Casa Renascer, Natal, BRAZIL
Caption: Colorful paints brighten the day—and face—of a girl in Brazil.
Photographer's Note: Natal is an all-year-long sunny city, located in northeastern Brazil. The place attracts visitors from all over the world looking for tropical beaches and a gentle people. I stayed there for one month working at Casa Renascer, an institution dedicated to taking care of at-risk girls and female teenagers who live in poverty, by providing them education, arts, and hope. As a photographer used to being with people from multiple backgrounds, those smiles confirmed my faith in our universal capacity to persist, and hopefully, succeed.
Credit Line: Ricardo Funari/BrazilPhotos/Alamy Ltd

Pg. 16 "Recess rocks"
Location: Lancaster, Pennsylvania, U.S.A.
Caption: Amish children play during recess at school.
Credit Line: Blair M. Seitz/Mira.com/drr.net

Pg. 17 "Lunch"
Location: New York, New York, U.S.A.
Caption: A group of kids chow down at lunchtime to fuel up for the afternoon.
Credit Line: Mario Tama/Getty Images

Pg. 18 "A little more learning"
Location: Seattle, Washington, U.S.A.
Caption: Computers are increasingly common in schools. The Internet connects kids from countries all over the world.
Credit Line: Andersen Ross/drr.net

Pg. 18 "Kids stand up, clean up"
Location: Jakarta, INDONESIA
Caption: A little girl helps tidy up at the end of the school day. In this economically depressed neighborhood, classes are held in an open-air school.
Credit Line: Reuters

Pg. 19 "Head for home"
Location: Portland, Oregon, U.S.A.
Caption: A girl skips across her school's blacktop after the final bell rings.
Photographer's Note: Before I made this photograph there had been rain for nine straight days (not uncommon in Portland), but seeing a possible change I quickly grabbed my camera, and left for my daughter's school. The bell rang and the children were released back to the world outside. The rain had stopped momentarily and the sun began to shine brightly onto the puddles of water. As I became mesmerized by the reflections, my daughter Malaya (her name means freedom), blissfully skipped across the playground. In her own way, she found the sun after the rain as compelling as I did.
Credit Line: Mark Downey/Lucid Images

Pg. 19 "Any way they can"
Location: New Delhi, INDIA
Caption: Tucked into every nook and cranny, more than 35 children ride a horse cart home from school.
Credit Line: Pawel Kopczynski/Reuters

Pgs. 20-21 "Kids work"
Location: The outskirts of Beza Mahafaly Special Reserve, MADAGASCAR
Caption: A Mahafaly boy drives a herd of zebu across a river. The cattle are known for their prominent humps and distinctive horns.
Photographer's Note: The humpbacked cattle called zebu nearly outnumber Madagascar's human population. They produce a relatively low yield of milk and meat, but are near sacred and generally are not eaten other than at ceremonies. They are a symbol of wealth and status. Zebu come in various colorations and there are at least 80 words in the Malagasy language to describe their attributes from color, horns, and hump.
Credit Line: Pete Oxford

Pg. 22 "Kids play"
Location: Mohini Village, INDIA
Caption: Children run through a field of yellow mustard flowers. Seeds from the plants are used to make mustard oil.
Photographer's Note: I went to take photographs of honey collectors in a mustard field during the winter season in northeast India. I noticed four young children playing in the vibrantly colorful field under bright sunshine. I didn't miss that beautiful opportunity and I started shooting. I learned that this moment of play was rare for these farmers' children, who break stones, collect sand from the river, search garbage for scrap materials, and do many other labors to help support their families. As a photographer it is always an immense pleasure to be a witness when nature plays with life.
Credit Line: Rupak De Chowdhuri/Reuters

Pg. 22 "With bats"
Location: Larkspur, Marin County, California, U.S.A.
Caption: Soy hot dogs satisfy a baseball team in California. Baseball has been played in America for over 150 years.
Credit Line: Catherine Karnow

Pg. 23 "And balls"
Location: Mumbai, INDIA
Caption: A line of batsmen prepare to score runs during cricket practice. The game was introduced to India in the 18th century by the British.
Credit Line: Catherine Karnow

Pg. 23 "And hoops"
Location: Khewra, PAKISTAN
Caption: A boy rolls a hoop down a cobblestone street. He keeps the hoop upright with strokes from a short stick.
Credit Line: Adrees Latif/Reuters

Pg. 23 "And slides"
Location: Baghdad, IRAQ
Caption: Children slip down a slide at a riverfront park in Baghdad. Years of war have made it difficult, at times, for kids to play outside.
Credit Line: Ceerwan Aziz/Reuters

Pg. 24 "Homework"
Location: Salta, ARGENTINA
Caption: Schoolgirls sit before a statue as they study in Salta. The city is famous for its colonial Spanish architecture.
Credit Line: John Hay/Lonely Planet

Pg. 24 "Chores"
Location: Golden, British Columbia, CANADA
Caption: A hungry horse appreciates a late afternoon snack.
Credit Line: Philip and Karen Smith/Iconica/Getty Images

Pg. 24 "Nothing at all"
Location: Austin Creek State Recreation Area, Sonoma County, California, U.S.A.
Caption: A young girl runs where a path leads in a recreation area in Northern California. Although close to urban development, the area is also home to many animals, including foxes, spotted owls, and bullfrogs.
Credit Line: Mark Downey/Lucid Images

Pg. 25 "Pondering life's big questions"
Location: Abidjan, IVORY COAST
Caption: Children play leapfrog on a huge pile of sand in Abidjan.
Photographer's Note: Children, as I always like to say, are another type of creature altogether. They're carefree, full of energy, and instinctually know to seize the day. For children, freedom—true freedom—is what guides their lives. In this picture taken on the building site of a bridge in a suburb of Abidjan where I was reporting, the kids are playing leapfrog on a pile of sand above the building site. I was afraid for them because it was a dangerous place next to these very heavy machines. But they seemed happy, happy because they were playing. I lost no time that day immortalizing the little ones absorbed in their games with that beautiful sky in the background, making for a great shot. I wanted to hold on to a memory of these children who had once again surprised me with their boundless freedom.
Credit Line: Thierry Gouegnon/Reuters

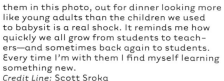
Pgs. 26-27 "What's for dinner?"
Location: Shiping Village, Yunnan Province, CHINA
Caption: A family enjoys a meal of pork, greens, and tofu. Tofu, a curd made from soybeans, has been eaten in China for over a thousand years.
Credit Line: Lynn Johnson/National Geographic

Pg. 28 "Veggies"
Location: Zhenfeng, Guizhou Province, CHINA
Caption: A boy eats vegetables with a pair of chopsticks. Chopsticks are used in many countries, including China, Japan, Korea, and Vietnam.
Credit Line: Danita Delimont/Alamy Ltd

Pg. 28 "Pasta"
Location: Pianosa, ITALY
Caption: A girl twirls up a forkful of pasta. To make pasta, a dough of flour, eggs, salt, and water is cut into strips and then boiled.
Credit Line: Catherine Karnow

Pg. 28 "Chicken"
Location: Madison, Georgia, U.S.A.
Caption: A boy bites into a crispy drumstick.
Credit Line: Patrick Molnar/Taxi/Getty Images

Pg. 28 "Rice"
Location: Kathmandu, NEPAL
Caption: Rice, egg, and fish fill the plate of a girl in Nepal. Instead of using utensils, many Nepalese eat with their right hand.
Credit Line: Anders Ryman/Corbis

Pg. 29 "Pizza"
Location: St. Pete Beach, Florida, U.S.A.
Caption: Pizza parlors are a favorite destination for many American families.
Photographer's Note: Taylor and Tavish are fraternal twins who are almost twelve years old. As close friends of their parents, my wife and I are fortunate to spend a lot of time with them. They attend the same elementary school that I did, and once asked me, "Did you have our teacher for third grade, too?" If I did have a class with her, she would have been a classmate, not the teacher. Seeing

them in this photo, out for dinner looking more like young adults than the children we used to babysit is a real shock. It reminds me how quickly we all grow from students to teachers—and sometimes back again to students. Every time I'm with them I find myself learning something new.
Credit Line: Scott Sroka

Pg. 30 "The sun is setting"
Location: Monteagle, Tennessee, U.S.A.
Caption: A young girl reaches out for a firefly. A chemical reaction called bioluminescence causes the firefly's abdomen to glow.
Photographer's Note: This picture of my daughter chasing a firefly was made as the result of a conversation with my wife, April. April grew up in the South and caught lightning bugs in her yard every summer evening. She asked me one day if I could take a picture of fireflies as they rise up out of the grass on a summer night. I took this as a challenge. After all I had spent years tackling difficult subjects for *National Geographic* magazine. This couldn't be more difficult than, say, my Poisonous Cave assignment in Mexico...So there I was in the front yard, chasing my daughter, armed with my camera. I pre-focused the lens to its minimum setting and didn't even look through the viewfinder. Three rolls of film, and happily, one frame came out that said what I wanted.
Credit Line: Stephen Alvarez

Pg. 31 "It's getting dark"
Location: Redding, Connecticut, U.S.A.
Caption: Warm lights welcome a family home at day's end.
Credit Line: Gabe Palmer/ Corbis

Pg. 32 "Families gather"
Location: Lincoln, Nebraska, U.S.A.
Caption: After dinner is the perfect time for a rough-and-tumble between father and son.
Photographer's Note: I recently met a man who is a banker in Lincoln. He had a great smile, and told me his name was "Solo." I liked him immediately and thought that he had a warm, interesting face. He had photos of his wife and kids on his desk, and they looked good too. As a visual guy, I'm always looking for good-looking,

real people to photograph close to home. The fact that Solo is black, and from Africa originally, and that his wife is a white woman from Nebraska, also intrigued me. I asked if I could spend a typical evening at home with them and give them free prints of anything that I shot. We set a date. The shoot went just fine, and they seemed very much at ease with me there. The kids were elated when Dad came home, then wouldn't eat dinner, which is typical. At dark they argued over who got to play with Daddy. After that, Solo read books and turned out the lights on kids still refusing to go to sleep. All in all, it seemed a lot like the way things operate at my house. The best part? I did this entire shoot in my own hometown, and got to sleep in my own bed that night. It doesn't get any better than that.
Credit Line: Joel Sartore

Pg. 33 "On the porch"
Location: Norfolk, Virginia, U.S.A.
Caption: A family rocks on the porch in Norfolk, where warm summer nights are tempered by cool breezes off the Chesapeake Bay.
Credit Line: Mark Edward Atkinson/drr.net

Pg. 33 "By the fire"
Location: Westport, Massachusetts, U.S.A.
Caption: Toasting marshmallows over an open fire is a popular camping activity.
Credit Line: Kindra Clineff/Index Stock Imagery/Jupiter Images

Pg. 34 "Family time"
Location: In the desert near the border with Iraq, SAUDI ARABIA
Caption: A grandfather plays a finger game with his grandchildren during a gathering of nomads in the Syrian desert.
Photographer's Note: In 2003, I was on a long assignment in Saudi Arabia for National Geographic. I'd heard about a large annual gathering of nomads and camels in the middle of nowhere in the Syrian Desert. Strange as it may sound, every year they hold a beauty contest for female camels, which draws thousands of men and animals. Some of them come from afar—even from neighboring countries. This aged grandfather had come from Qatar. I asked him why he had brought his family with him, and he replied, "I brought the children so they could see this meeting of nomads and take part in it. So they

could experience living in a tent in the desert for a few days, like their ancestors before them. We are nomads — the children need to see for themselves what being a nomad means." The grandfather's wise words reminded me that parents and grandparents the world over have the responsibility of passing on their traditions and knowledge to the next generations.
Credit Line: Reza/National Geographic

Pg. 35 "Quiet time"
Location: Bedugul, Bali, INDONESIA
Caption: Boys pray in a mosque. Many Muslims pray at least five times a day, including at nightfall.
Credit Line: Abbas/Magnum Photos

Pg. 36 "Brush teeth"
Location: Tiburon, California, U.S.A.
Caption: A mother and son clown around while brushing their teeth.
Photographer's Note: The youngest of four kids, four-year-old Wilder plays around with mom, Kimberly Brooks, at teeth-brushing time. I spent a day with Kimberly and her four kids and decided that she was what I would call a "cool" mom. She drives not an SUV, but a VW bug; she plays Black-Eyed Peas at breakfast and dances with her kids in the kitchen. The walls in the house are all painted different bright colors. She grew up in Northern California in the hippie era, and brings the ideals of those times into her life now. That she is both a homemaker and a cool mom makes her very much an American mother of today. She plays a lot with her kids and tries to make each day fun for everyone.
Credit Line: Catherine Karnow

Pg. 36 "One more story"
Location: Allentown, Pennsylvania, U.S.A.
Caption: A girl snuggles close to hear a good story. In many American families, bedtime stories are a nightly ritual.
Photographer's Note: Maureen brought her daughter Aminah in from a summer day of sun and sprinklers in the backyard. I spent the afternoon trying to fix some of that afternoon's gold and her daughter's smile in a few frames of film. Conversation touched on memories of Brooklyn, thoughts of a trip to Sicily, and now the languid ease of their Pennsylvania garden. With the sun now lost to another side of the Earth's curve, Aminah unwound in Maureen's lap for her ritual of a story before bed. Earlier

in the afternoon, I chased color, cartwheels, and summer dresses with a camera, and yet here, at the end of the day, stopping this moment in a photograph felt like the only thing that mattered. I could think of nothing else. Here they eclipsed even the sun: this mother, her daughter, and their book.
Credit Line: Omar Mullick

Pg. 37 "Kiss goodnight"
Location: New York, New York, U.S.A.
Caption: A little girl and her dog grab some shut-eye at the end of the day.
Credit Line: Elliott Erwitt/ Magnum Photos

Pg. 38 "Kids dream"
Location: Amazonas, BRAZIL
Caption: Two hammocks make for cozy beds on a riverboat in Brazil. Families living near the Amazon river often travel by riverboat.
Photographer's Note: Amazonian families travel constantly, to work, reunite with other parts of the family, visit the nearest doctor or hospital....or go shopping. Just as they do anywhere I suppose. The difference here is that it takes days. Nobody wears a watch or cares much about the passage of time in Amazonas, they don't listen to the weather forecast and don't concern themselves much with privacy. Life on the Amazon lilts gently along, rather like the languid and fluid motions of the riverboat, intertwining inevitably and uncontrollably as the various branches of the Amazon River. The hammock was surely invented for such a place, and it is inconceivable for locals to travel without one. The children—a brother and sister—are as contented as any children I ever saw. Cocooned in their slings for comfort and warmth, they while away the hours gliding down the mightiest river on the planet.
Credit Line: Jeremy Horner

Pg. 39 "All the possibilities"
Location: Montepulciano, Tuscany, ITALY
Caption: A girl looks out at the Tuscan fields from her bedroom window, wondering what the day will bring.
Photographer's Note: Last summer we traveled with friends to the Tuscan countryside. Their daughter, then 11 years old, reflected a perfect blend of precocious interest in an old, romantic culture with pure, present enjoyment of tangible details like shopping, or

the perfect pizza, or the steamy sun. One day I passed by her room and caught her on the open windowsill, quiet and still. She glowed, at home in herself in a new place, without the distractions of the familiar. The Italian way had illuminated in her corners I had yet to meet; and I think she saw herself differently for a time, too. And this is what I want for my own child—the mirror of a world beyond his home to challenge what he knows about himself and others, and reflective moments in new spaces to nurture acceptance of what is and what's possible.
Credit Line: Heather Perry/National Geographic

Pgs. 40-41 "One day"
Location: Velenje, SLOVENIA
Caption: Children soar high on a flying carousel.
Credit Line: Srdjan Zivulovic/Reuters

Pg. 48
Location: PAPUA NEW GUINEA
Caption: Dancers—with bubblegum—pose during the Mt. Hagen Cultural Show, a dance and music festival that brings together members from Papua New Guinea's 700 indigenous tribes.
Credit Line: Cristina Mittermeier

Back cover, left
Location: Bimini Islands, BAHAMA ISLANDS
Caption: Where the forest meets the ocean, a child plays on the beach.
Credit Line: James L. Stanfield/National Geographic

Back cover, center
Location: Mandalay, MYANMAR
Caption: A girl wears thanakha powder to protect and beautify her skin.
Credit Line: Bruno Morandi

Back cover, right
Location: Red Square, Moscow, RUSSIA
Caption: Sparklers light up the new year for a child at Red Square in Moscow. People have been visiting Red Square for centuries.
Credit Line: Tatyana Makeyeva/Reuters

ARCTIC OCEAN

U.S.

CANADA

NORTH AMERICA

RUSSIA

A S I A

EUROPE

A little more learning, p.18
Seattle, Washington

head for home, p.19
Portland, Oregon

nothing at all, p.24
Sonoma County, California

baseball, p.22
Larkspur, California

Brush teeth, p.36
Tiburon, California

Science projects, p.15
Hermosa Beach, California

chores, p.24
Golden, British Columbia, Canada

One more story, p.36
Allentown, Pennsylvania

It's getting dark, p.31
Redding, Connecticut

Families gather, p.32
Lincoln, Nebraska

UNITED STATES

Get up, p.6
St. Louis, Missouri

The sun is setting, p.30
Monteagle, Tennessee

Chicken, p.28
Madison, Georgia

Pizza, p.29
St. Pete Beach, Florida

Back cover (left)
Bimini Islands, Bahamas

By the fire, p.33
Westport, Massachusetts

Lunch, p.17 and
Kiss goodnight, p.37
New York, New York

By bus, p.13
Doylestown, Pennsylvania

Recess rocks, p.16
Lancaster, Pennsylvania

on porches, p.33
Norfolk, Virginia

Pancakes, p.8
Sevierville, Tennessee

BAHAMAS

ATLANTIC OCEAN

Pasta, p.28
Pienza, Italy

one day, pp.40–41
Velenje, Slovenia

SLOVENIA

SPAIN

ITALY

all the possibilities, p.39
Montepulciano, Italy

Churros, p.8
Granada, Spain

AFRICA

celebrate a new day, p.7
Kadesh Barnea, Israel

ISRAEL

IRAQ

and slides, p.23
Baghdad, Iraq

Family time, p.34
Saudi Arabia

SAUDI ARABIA

and hoops, p.23
Khewra, Pakistan

PAKISTAN

any way they can, p.19
New Delhi, India

NEPAL

CHINA

Rice, p.28
Kathmandu, Nepal

NORTH KOREA

Porridge, p.8
Wonsan, North Korea

Music, p.14
Shanghai, China

Real adventure, p.12
Gongshan County, China

Veggies, p.28
Zhenfeng, China

What's for dinner?, pp.26–27
Shiping, China

GUINEA-BISSAU

Half-title and
Wash up, p.6
Dembel Jumpora, Guinea-Bissau

SIERRA LEONE

Math, p.15
Sussex, Sierra Leone

CÔTE D'IVOIRE
(IVORY COAST)

Pondering life's questions, p.25
Abidjan, Côte D'Ivoire

Kids dream, p.38
Amazonas, Brazil

Arts and crafts, p.15
Casa Renascer, Natal, Brazil

BRAZIL

SOUTH AMERICA

BOLIVIA

By bike, p.13
Oruro, Bolivia

homework, p.24
Salta, Argentina

ARGENTINA

PACIFIC OCEAN

KENYA

Reading, p.14
Bahati, Kenya

MADAGASCAR

Kids work, pp.20–21
southwestern Madagascar

INDIAN OCEAN

Short walk, p.12
Jodhpur, India

INDIA

Time for school, pp.10–11
Ahmadabad, India

cricket, p.22
Mumbai, India

At dawn, pp.4–5
Kerala, India

Title page and
Back cover (center)
Mandalay, Myanmar

MYANMAR (BURMA)

Hot sweet tea, p.9
Azmiriganj, Bangladesh

BANGLADESH

Kids play, p.22
Mohini village, India

CAMBODIA

Un toot, p.13
and Writing, p.14
Hani village, China

Front cover
Phnom Penh, Cambodia

PACIFIC OCEAN

kids stand up, clean up, p.18
Jakarta, Indonesia

INDONESIA

Quiet time, p.35
Bedugul, Indonesia

PAPUA NEW GUINEA

Author's dedication,
Papua New Guinea

AUSTRALIA

Toast, p.8
Cremorne, Australia

MAP KEY

Country where book photo originated

By bike, p.13
Oruro, Bolivia

Description, page number, and location of photo

Dedication: To Pam, Susan,
Mary... and cake!

ACKNOWLEDGMENTS Many thanks to the following people, who took
210 words on a plain white piece of paper, and turned them into so
much more:

Jennifer Emmett, executive editor

Bea Jackson, art direction / design

Lori Epstein, photo editor

David Seager and Jim Hiscott, design

Jennifer Eaton, editorial assistant

Grace Hill, managing editor

Carl Mehler and Nicholas P. Rosenbach, map design

NOTE The black-and-white photography in the book is the artistic
choice of the photographer, except on pages 8, 17, 22, and 28 where
images were digitally converted for pacing.

Text copyright © 2009 Barbara Kelly

Published by the National Geographic Society.
All rights reserved.
Reproduction of the whole or any part of the contents
without written permission from the National Geographic Society
is strictly prohibited.

The text of the book is set in Tarzana Wide
by Zuzana Licko from Emigre

Library of Congress Cataloging-in-Publication Data

Kerley, Barbara.
One world, one day / Barbara Kerley.
ISBN 978-1-4263-0460-6 (hardcover : alk. paper) — ISBN 978-1-
4263-0461-3 (library binding : alk. paper)
1. Children—Social life and customs—Juvenile literature. 2.
Children—Pictorial works—Juvenile literature. I. Title.
HQ781.5.K47 2008
305.23409—dc22
2008029315

Founded in 1888, the National Geographic society
is one of the largest scientific and educational
organizations in the world. It reaches more than
285 million people worldwideeach month through
its official journal, NATIONAL GEOGRAPHIC, and its
four other magazines; The National Geographic
Channel; television documentaries; radio
programs; films; books; videos and DVDs; maps; and interactive
media. National Geographic has funded more than 8,000 scientific
research projects and supports an education program combating
geographic illiteracy.

For more information please call 1-800-NGS-LINE (647-5463)
Or write to the following address:

NATIONAL GEOGRAPHIC SOCIETY
1145 17th Street N.W.
Washington, D.C. 20036-4688 U.S.A.
Visit the Society's Web site:
www.nationalgeographic.com/books

Printed in the United States of America